Reviews &

"...A superb manual which makes the case for self-publishing and demonstrates that it is possible to go head to head against the Big Boys and come out a winner... Easy to read and wonderfully complete in its concepts and introductory information, this book is encouraging and truthful. We rated it five hearts."

— Bob Spear, Publisher and Chief Reviewer, *Heartland Reviews*

"GREAT NEW BOOK ABOUT SELF-PUBLISHING...doesn't disappoint. Poynter and Snow provide detailed, practical advice on self-publishing..."

— Tim Bete, Erma Bombeck Writers' Workshop, University of Dayton

"Poynter and Snow: a tremendous team. Both are great writers and they know the publishing business, both electronic and print."

— Randy "Dr. Proactive" Gilbert, Author of *Success Bound*

"...if you want a quick read and self-publishing information in a nutshell, this is the book for you... The book is written in an easy to follow style and, between the book and the Web site, nearly all of your self-publishing questions are addressed."

— Patricia Fry, Small Publishers, Artists and Writers Network

"An absolute "must-have" for anyone with a book inside just waiting to get out... enthusiastically recommended..."

— Jim Cox, *Midwest Book Review*

"If you are interested [in] an alternative way to get your book(s) out there, this book will get you started in the right direction."

— Dr. Tag Powell, National Association of Independent Publishers

U-Publish.com 4.0

U-Publish.com 4.0:
A 'Living Book' to Help You Compete with the Giants of Publishing

**Dan Poynter
and
Danny O. Snow**

Revised and updated for 2007 and beyond

Unlimited Publishing LLC
Bloomington, Indiana

Copyright © 2007 by Dan Poynter and Danny O. Snow

Distributing Publisher: Unlimited Publishing LLC, www.UnlimitedPublishing.com, P.O. Box 3007, Bloomington, IN 47402-3007, Tel. 800-218-8877.

Contributing Publishers: Dan Poynter, www.ParaPublishing.com, P.O Box 8206, Santa Barbara, CA 93118-8206 and Danny O. Snow, www.U-Publish.com, P.O. Box 99, Nashville, IN 47448.

Excerpts from *Book Marketing: A New Approach* Copyright © 1988-2006 by Dan Poynter, used by permission. Rights to material excerpted from articles by Danny O. Snow in *BookTech Magazine*, *The PMA Independent* and other publications reverted to the writer on publication, now Copyright © 2000-2007 by Danny O. Snow and used by permission.

All rights reserved under Title 17, U.S. Code, International and Pan-American Copyright Conventions. No part of this work may be reproduced or transmitted in any form or by any means, electronic or mechanical, including photocopying, scanning, recording, narration, broadcast or live performance, or duplication by any information storage or retrieval system, without prior written permission from the author(s) and publisher(s), except for brief quotations with attribution in a review or report. Please visit the distributing publisher's Web site at http://www.UnlimitedPublishing.com for more information.

Unlimited Publishing LLC ("UP") provides worldwide book design, production, marketing and distribution services for professional authors and publishers, serving as distributing publisher. Sole responsibility for the content of each work rests with the author(s) and/or contributing publisher(s). Information or opinions expressed herein do not originate from UP, nor any of its officers, contractors, affiliates, agents or assigns.

This book is sold contingent on the reader's prior agreement that the author(s) and publisher(s) are not rendering legal, accounting or other professional services of any kind, nor endorsing any of the referenced resources. It is not the purpose of this report to provide all the information that is available to readers elsewhere, but to complement, amplify and supplement other texts. For more information, see the many references. Every effort has been made to make this report as complete and as accurate as possible, but it may contain errors both typographical and in content. Therefore, this book should be used only as a general overview and not as a definitive source of information. The author(s) and publisher(s) accept no responsibility of any kind for any loss or damage caused or alleged to be caused directly or indirectly by the information contained herein. If you do not agree with the terms above, you may return this book in good condition for a full refund.

Fourth Edition
Library of Congress Control Number:
2006934493

ISBN:
1-58832-175-4 or 978-1-58832-175-6 (Paperback)
1-58832-176-2 or 978-1-58832-176-6 (Hardback)

Copies of this fine book and many others are available to order at:
http://www.unlimitedpublishing.com

Table of Contents

ACKNOWLEDGEMENTS 1

PREFACE BY DAN POYNTER 3

PREFACE BY DANNY O. SNOW 5

INTRODUCTION 7

CHAPTER 1: WHY SELF-PUBLISH? 11

CHAPTER 2: BEFORE YOU START WRITING 17

CHAPTER 3: THINK AHEAD AS YOU WRITE! 21

CHAPTER 4: PUBLISHING METHODS: SELF-PUBLISHING VERSUS
VANITY PUBLISHING 27

CHAPTER 5: PRINTING METHODS: POD, DIGITAL SHORT RUN AND
OFFSET PRINTING 29

CHAPTER 6: FROM MANUSCRIPT TO GALLEY 33

CHAPTER 7: FROM GALLEY TO BOOK 39

CHAPTER 8: IN PRINT AT LAST 43

CHAPTER 9: TRADITIONAL MARKETS 47

CHAPTER 10: NON-TRADITIONAL MARKETS 51

CHAPTER 11: ONLINE MARKETING 55

CHAPTER 12: AFTERWORD 61

APPENDIX: THE "LIVING BOOK" 63

Acknowledgements

Dan Poynter thanks his tireless staff for making his office run so that he may devote his full energies to writing, promoting and his clients.

Danny O. Snow dedicates his work on this edition to his fiancée Jenny, and gratefully acknowledges the support and encouragement he has received over many years from the late William Alfred; Sam Ardery; Dr. S.I. Ball et. al.; Ted Bayliss; BCS Advertising's Jeanette Brown and Paul Smedberg; Holly Blatman; *BookTech Magazine's* Gretchen Kirby, Donna Loyle and colleagues; Tom Buckner; Mark Butler; the Carey-Davis family; the Carlson family; the Childress family; Frank DeFord; Richard Adrian Dorr; *eBookWeb* founders Wade Roush and Glenn Sanders; Mary Frances England; Burl Frame; Chuck and Robin Harris; John Hartley; John William Houghton; David Jeffers and family; L. Bruce Jones; Florrie Binford Kichler; Charles King; Mary Kramer; Larry Larkin; Chuck Loesche; Rock Lofton and Coco; The Clan MacAaron; John Mace; Jack Magestro and his colleagues, canine and human; Bruce Moffitt and family; Richard Eoin Nash; Mark O'Donnell; *PMA's* Judith Appelbaum, Jan and Terry Nathan and colleagues; Tony Ratliff; Wade Roush; Glenn Sanders; Robert Burns Shaw; the Shartiag family; Dave Shearer; Jane Shore; assorted Snows and Parkhouses; Mathijs Suidman; Rick Sutton; Mark Swisher; Greg Temple; Doug Warner; Bob Zaltsberg, and of course, his #1 fans (who also happen to be his parents) Harry David and Jeanne L. Snow. He also extends special thanks to co-author Dan Poynter for the opportunity to collaborate with the recognized leader in the field of self-publishing.

Thousands of readers of previous editions also deserve our gratitude. Corrections, updates, debates, and most of all *new ideas from readers* have been invaluable in shaping the material presented here. While we hope that our readers learn from our books, we also learn from our readers, and welcome their input.

A final note of appreciation goes to Leslie Komet Ausburn, executive producer of the popular *Ask Heloise* radio show. Her invitation to join our favorite "hintologist" and her millions of listeners on a nationally-syndicated broadcast in August 2004 provided the initial motivation to prepare new editions for publication in 2005 and 2007.

Preface by Dan Poynter

Writing the book is just the beginning — the proverbial tip of the iceberg. A larger investment of time and money must be made once the manuscript is completed. Promotion is the part of the iceberg that is under the water. Many authors do not see the submerged part and do not even realize it is there.

As an author, you have the responsibilities of a parent. Your book is a new member of your family. You are giving birth to it and now you must raise it. Books cannot flourish on their own;

they need a lot of parental guidance and nurturing time. Fortunately, your book is not a 20-year commitment and you do not have to send it to college... but you do have to invest time and money to bring it up.

It does not matter if you sell your manuscript to a publisher or publish it yourself; the author must do the promotion. It is sad that authors must learn this over and over: *Publishers do not promote books*. They get the books into stores and they list the books in their catalogs, period. Authors must get the customers into the stores to pull the books through the system. So, whether you are an author-publisher or only an author, this book is for you.

Watch your money. Do the free and inexpensive promotion first. Use e-mail rather than envelopes and stamps; send copies to book reviewers and stage local autographings and mini seminars.

Make up your promotion plan: read this book and fill in the plan. Prioritize the ideas, placing the most important ones first. Then work your way through the list. If you have a day job or some other activity to occupy part of your day, it will take you longer to get through the list. But you will be secure in the knowledge that you are doing all the right things to promote your book, and that you are doing them in the right order.

— Dan Poynter
September, 2004

Preface by Danny O. Snow

The first paperback edition of *U-Publish.com* was released in January 2000. Strictly speaking, the 21st Century didn't start until a year later, but nevertheless Dan Poynter and I felt it a fitting publication date. After all, we were predicting how books would be published in the new millennium.

Six years and three editions later, we have the benefits of hindsight, subsequent experimentation, and more innovations in technology... plus many new ideas from of readers of previous editions, for which we are deeply grateful. We learn a lot from our readers, and value your input.

Readers of previous editions will notice that this one is shorter. Times have changed; in 2000 it seemed bold to tie the content of a paperback book to a Web site, monthly e-mail updates, and other features that are now considered almost routine. Today, we no longer waste paper and ink to print lists of book designers, distributors, editors, printers, promoters and other resources, only to see some listings change by the time the book is publicly released. Instead, the many lists and links printed in early editions are now maintained at the Web site named for the book (www.U-Publish.com) where they are updated periodically, to keep readers up-to-date long after our printed editions go to press. After you have finished reading this book, be sure to check online for updates regularly, in order to get the latest information available!

In the same spirit, you will find an appendix at the back of this book that includes monthly updates from our e-mail newsletters. New items will be added every month, making the book grow over time. This strategy adds to our "living book" philosophy, giving readers fresh new material on a regular basis.

We are confident that major publishers will increasingly adopt new methods of book production, distribution and marketing in the years ahead, as outlined in previous editions and expanded in this one.

Meanwhile, self-publishing authors and independent publishers are leading the way. *Nearly any good book with a clear audience can be successfully published by its author*, using new technologies to slash costs and reach readers more directly. By following the strategies in this book, you can be part of a real revolution in the world of publishing — a revolution that is already underway.

— Danny O. Snow
September, 2006

Introduction

The publishing industry is changing dramatically in the 21st Century. New methods of printing and distributing books, changes in business models used by authors, publishers and booksellers, and the ability of writers to reach readers directly over the Internet, are re-defining the word "publish" in the new millennium.

Traditionally, less than 5% of all books written were ever published. This changed rapidly as new technologies made it faster and more economical to publish books.

By 2004, the number of new books published soared to an all-time high of 195,000 titles in a single year. A record number of them were self-published. Why? The answers are only partially related to new technologies; sociological and economic factors also influenced the direction of the publishing world.

A major transformation in the music industry began a few years ago, as recording artists began to abandon major record labels in favor of distributing directly to the public. Many musicians went independent not only because music could now be easily downloaded from the Internet, but also because the major labels overcharged consumers and underpaid artists for years. The labels, not the artists, decided which songs would be released. Artists were often sent on lengthy road tours to boost record sales, while the labels reaped the rewards. These factors and others drove recording artists away.

Musicians who distribute directly to the public enjoy greater artistic control, and a greater share of revenues. Given the advantages of independent distribution and the adversarial relationships between musicians and music labels, who can blame artists for jumping ship?

We are now seeing a similar pattern follow in the book world, for reasons less severe but still related.

Starting in the 1980s, major publishers focused more and more on mass-market books that sold millions of copies, often at the expense of books with legitimate literary merit but more modest commercial potential. The big publishing houses went fishing for the next Harry Potter and threw back the rest without much patience.

In fairness to the big New York houses, let's admit what few writers recognize: more than 95% of books from traditional publishers never recover the author's advance — let alone earn a profit. Major publishers need big bestsellers to cover their costs for the rest. Nevertheless, the focus of big publishers on mass appeal drives many writers of worthwhile (but less commercial) books to look for alternatives.

Simultaneously, new methods of book production, distribution and promotion now make it cost-effective to produce books in infinitely smaller quantities — even one at a time.

More than ever before, leading publishers could keep nearly any worthy book in print profitably, including those that sell only a few hundred copies per year. But many major publishers simply aren't very interested in small profits from books that sell moderately but consistently over time.

Bookstore chains add to the problem, with a "move 'em in, move 'em out" philosophy that highlights a handful of hot new titles on bookstore shelves each week, often overlooking good books that sell less briskly.

This is a shame for everyone: the reader, the writer and the publisher. It drives larger publishers to focus more on good numbers than good words. It encourages mediocrity and complaisance rather than risk-taking and innovation. It gives relatively few new writers a chance — and those who are published by the leading publishers often see their books fall out-of-print all too soon.

So we now see a convergence of factors where many larger publishers neglect good books for economic rather than literary reasons, while writers scramble to carve out niche markets on their own.

The result is a boom in self-publishing: *Nearly any good book with a clearly identifiable audience can be successfully published by the author,* using new technologies to lower costs and reach readers more directly. We predict that major publishers will eventually adopt many of the methods outlined here. In the interim, thousands of writers are already exploiting them, with more joining the ranks every day. You can be one of them.

Chapter 1: Why Self-Publish?

"...Self-publishing is much easier now," said Calvin Reid, an editor at *Publishers Weekly*. "Before, you had to spend thousands of dollars. Now you can have your book wonderfully published for several hundred dollars and print on demand." Add to that, "conscientious, relentless marketing," Mr. Reid said, "and you have a recipe for success."
— *The New York Times*, 9/8/2004

Self-publishing (also called independent publishing or alternative publishing) offers many benefits to writers: more control of content, a bigger share of profits, faster publication, and greater potential to tap lucrative specialty markets beyond bookstores and libraries.

The benefits of more editorial control and more money are fairly self-evident. The benefits of exploiting non-traditional markets are less obvious, but equally important.

In a 1996 report, the Book Industry Study Group (BISG.org), a leading book trade association for policy, standards and research, estimated that there are nearly TEN TIMES more outlets for books than bookstores *per se*. These markets are far more numerous, easier to target, often pay more and pay faster than conventional book trade channels.

In his 'special report' titled *Book Marketing: A New Approach*, Dan Poynter wrote "It is suspected that a very large, unreported number [of books] are sold through specialty shops... catalogs, as premiums, etc. These non-traditional sales are usually easier to make, very large and much more lucrative."

A subsequent BISG study in 2005 confirmed Poynter's suspicions by documenting that "smaller" publishers (those with annual revenues under $50 million) now generate *$11.5 billion per year in sales*, often reaching readers beyond the bookstore world — in many cases selling more books outside traditional trade channels than within.

"Since so many smaller publishers operate under the radar of traditional tracking mechanisms, it's been tempting in the past to think of them as 'regional' or 'niche,' and to assume that they're responsible for a small fraction of book sales in the market," said BISG Executive Director, Jeff Abraham. "Our new study shows that this kind of thinking won't fly in the future."

Books are now sold almost everywhere: in gift shops, supermarkets, airports, truck stops, and most importantly in vast numbers of stores with specialized product lines that are often compatible with a particular book's subject. No kidding: we've seen books about fishing selling like hotcakes off a rickety wooden pier on a remote stretch of the inter-coastal waterway, miles from the nearest town... and farther from the nearest bookstore!

The traditional publishing industry supplies a few specialty outlets as a sideline, but sells the majority of its books through major chain bookstores and libraries.

The terms for mainstream book trade sales are less than ideal for the publisher, conventional or independent. Mainstream booksellers expect big discounts, a long time to pay, and the right to return unsold books to the publisher on a routine basis. The sad fact is that bookstores rarely BUY books; instead, they take them on consignment!

On the other hand, non-traditional outlets are far more numerous, easier to identify, often pay more, pay faster, and return fewer (if any) unsold books. While conventional publishers move most of their inventory through mainstream channels, the savvy self-publisher can usually find better outlets.

To illustrate, suppose you have written a book about a relatively narrow subject like organic fertilizers... how many casual bookstore customers are interested in this subject? Probably very few. But now imagine the customers of a tree nursery or gardening supply center: *nearly ALL of them are potential readers!*

Traditional publishers generally don't even try to sell books in outlets like these, but self-publishers can take advantage of specialty markets that are often neglected by conventional publishers.

Conventional publishers tend to look down on non-traditional markets and self-published books. Often they cite frequent writing errors, amateurish layouts and cover designs, or other problems that are seldom seen in books from major publishers. Frankly, this attitude is sometimes justified — especially by marginal books from vanity presses — BUT *there is absolutely no reason why a self-published book can't meet professional standards.* To illustrate, here are just a handful of books that were originally self-published:

- *What Color is Your Parachute?* by Richard Nelson Bolles: originally published by the author, it has enjoyed more than 22 editions, 5 million copies and 288 weeks on the bestseller lists. It is now the "evergreen" title of respected publisher Ten Speed Press.

- *In Search of Excellence* by Tom Peters: more than 25,000 copies were sold directly to consumers in its first year. Then it was sold to Warner, which sold 10 million more.

- *Real Peace* by Richard M. Nixon.

- *The Celestine Prophecy* by James Redfield: his manuscript made the rounds of the mainstream houses, and then he decided to publish it himself. He started by selling copies out of the trunk of his Honda — more than 100,000 of them. He subsequently sold out to Warner for $800,000. The #1 bestseller in 1996, it has now sold at least 5 million copies, probably more.

- *The One-Minute Manager* by Ken Blanchard and Spencer Johnson: sold more than 20,000 copies locally before they sold out to Morrow. It has sold more than 12 million copies since 1982 and been translated in 25 languages.

- *A Time to Kill* by John Grisham.

- *The Joy of Cooking* by Irma Rombauer: this classic was self-published in 1931 as a project of the First Unitarian Women's Alliance in St. Louis. Today Scribner sells more than 100,000 copies each year.

- *The Lazy Man's Way to Riches*, by Joe Karbo, who never courted bookstores, and never sold out to a major publisher. He sold books directly to readers with ads in newspapers and magazines.

Other well-known self-publishers include: William Blake, Stephen Crane, e.e. cummings, Deepak Chopra, Benjamin Franklin, Zane Grey, James Joyce, Rudyard Kipling, D.H. Lawrence, Thomas Paine, Edgar Allen Poe, Ezra Pound, Carl Sandburg, George Bernard Shaw, Upton Sinclair, Gertrude Stein, Henry David Thoreau, Mark Twain, Walt Whitman and Virginia Woolf... to name just a few.

So don't tell us that a self-published book can't meet (or beat) the standards of conventional publishers! If you have the *passion* to write about a subject you love, the *time and skills* to prepare a quality book for publication, the *confidence* to take some financial risks, and most of all the *determination* to promote and market your book proactively, you can self-publish successfully.

For those who do, this book will briefly summarize the most important things you can do to succeed, and some pitfalls to avoid.

Chapter 2: Before You Start Writing

Don't write a book first, then try to find readers for it. Instead, target your readers *before you start writing*. Study other books on your subject at libraries, bookstores and online. Fill a need that isn't already met, or do a better job meeting the need than other writers. Books that are unique have an advantage, but nearly *any quality book with a clearly defined audience can be successfully self-published.*

Observe whether comparable books are paperbacks or hardbacks, how many pages they contain, their prices, and how they look. Plan yours to be truly competitive in each respect when it is published.

Novels and poetry are tougher than non-fiction, because it is harder to pinpoint the audience for general fiction than to identify readers for a book about a specific, practical topic. But even a first novel or book of verse can be successful, if you plan carefully beforehand, work hard (and work smart) to promote it after publication, and use your creativity in marketing as much as writing.

Before you start writing for self-publication, read books by experts. Books by experts provide insights drawn from years of experience that you can absorb in a week or two. A single good tip from a book like this can save you *many times* the cost of buying it.

The Self-Publishing Manual by co-author Dan Poynter is generally considered "the bible for self-publishers." It is available at most libraries and bookstores, or at ParaPublishing.com — with a ton of online resources, many of which are free. It has helped literally thousands of writers to publish books independently.

There are many more good books about self-publishing — too many to cover here. To recommend just two, read *Beyond the Bookstore* by Brian Jud, and *The Publishing Game* by Fern Reiss. John Kremer (BookMarket.com) has several books about marketing that are excellent... And let's not forget some great online newsletters by Jim Barnes at IndependentPublisher.com and of course "Publishing Poynters," the #1 newsletter for self-publishers, available free at ParaPublishing.com.

Another way to gain expertise is to join a trade association such as PMA, the Independent Publishers Association (PMA-Online.org); The Small Publishers Association of North America (SPANnet.org); and The Small Publishers, Artists and Writers Network (Spawn.org). These groups provide many opportunities for education, and they are exceptionally welcoming to newcomers. PMA, for example, holds an annual "Publishing University" where you can attend highly informative workshops and seminars that are ideal for the new publisher. It's hard to overstate the benefits of membership for those getting started in publishing.

After you've finished reading what the experts say, talk to a book designer and a printer, to learn the best ways to prepare your manuscript.

A reminder for readers: many resources cited here are available online, and updated periodically. This helps us keep readers up-to-date long after each edition goes to press. Another tip: we don't endorse specific products or services, nor do we accept fees for mentioning them. Resources are provided simply as a starting point for your own research, and we strongly encourage you to research several other sources before making decisions about publishing a book.

For a preliminary list of book designers, visit
***U-Publish.com/design* and other sources**

For an introductory list of printers, visit
***U-Publish.com/print* and other sources**

An experienced book designer can explain things like why each chapter should start on a right-hand page, or why faces in a photo should be at least as big as a dime. A professional printer can show you how to save money if your completed book fits a particular number of pages in a particular trim size, or how to arrange colored pages (if any) inside a book for the lowest possible print cost. This information can guide you in preparing the manuscript for the best results.

Throughout the process of self-publishing, don't hesitate to *get professional help when needed.* It's called self-publishing, but this *doesn't* mean you need to do everything yourself! This is especially true for things you aren't fully qualified to do. Today, it's possible to produce a quality book at a fraction of the cost of traditional publishing, even budgeting for professional assistance. You'll probably spend hundreds of hours writing and preparing your book for publication — don't throw away your time and money by refusing to pay for qualified help in key areas and ending up with a sub-standard book. Think of yourself as a general contractor building a house: You're in charge, but of course you job out the wiring to an electrician, rather than trying to do it yourself. As a publisher, use specialists in editorial work, typesetting and printing unless by chance you're an expert yourself.

Budget accordingly. In very round numbers, for a 200-page paperback, a conventional publisher would probably invest almost $10,000, starting with an initial printing of 3,000 or more copies. For a comparable book, a self-publisher using Print-on-Demand (POD) can often get started for less than $1,000 plus the cost of printing 100 to 500 copies initially.

If you invest $2,000 and earn $5 from each sale, you'll need 400 sales to achieve profitability. The good news is that nearly any worthwhile book can sell 400 copies — often *many times* more! The following chapters will show you how.

Chapter 3: Think Ahead as You Write!

Write about a subject you know well, and one that you enjoy. This will not only make the process of publishing more pleasant, but more profitable, as we will explain.

Especially, begin writing with a specific plan that includes the topic, market(s) and physical description of the book. For example: "My goal is to write a paperback book about organic fertilizers that I will sell for $14.99 at gardening centers, tree nurseries, flower shows, horticulture clubs, from my own Web site and with a limited amount of direct mail. It will be about 15,000 words (or 100 pages) in length, 6x9" trim size, with a full color cover, black-and-white interior, a few illustrations, index and bibliography."

Pick a style manual, such as the *AP Stylebook* or *Chicago Manual of Style* (available at most libraries and bookstores) and follow the guidelines consistently. For example, when a quotation ends with a question, does the question mark appear inside the quotation marks, or outside? Either way is OK, but the manuscript should be 100% consistent throughout.

A big part of writing well is economy of style: express your points clearly and simply, with as many words as needed, but not a single word more. Economy of style will later translate to economy of budget, reducing your editing costs, typesetting and layout costs, printing costs, shipping costs, and more. In the long run, writing 20 extra pages that are not essential will add to your publication expenses and do a disservice to your readers.

Work with an editor, or at least a qualified proofreader — someone with a working background in spelling and grammar. This is true even if you are a gifted writer; authors are often so close to their own work that they overlook problems that might seem obvious to an outsider.

For a short list of common writing problems, and editors who can fix them for a fee, see:

U-Publish.com/edit and other sources

A few more suggestions are explained below, but please note that they are *not a substitute* for a comprehensive style guide or a qualified proofreader. Please do not take offense if these examples seem elementary to you! Our intention is to err on the side of caution, even for seasoned writers who probably take the following items for granted.

Use numbers consistently. For example, you may want to spell out numbers from one through ten, but use numerals for 11 and higher. It is acceptable to use a different convention, provided usage is 100% consistent throughout.

Spoken dialogue is typically surrounded by quotation marks, with each speaker's words treated as a paragraph. For a simple example, see the conversation below:

"How do we handle dialogue?" the writer asked.
"Like this," the editor replied.

For longer speeches, in which a person speaks more than one paragraph, open the speech with a quotation mark, but do not close the quotation at the end of the first paragraph. Begin the second paragraph with an open quotation mark. When the entire speech is completed, use a close quotation mark. For example:

An author might ask "How do we handle quotations that are longer than a single paragraph? Is it better to close the quotation at the end of each sentence, each paragraph, or what?

"After reading this example, I understand that it is better not to close the quotation until the speaker has finished talking, even when the quotation spans more than one paragraph."

Do NOT capitalize entire words, unless there is an exceptional reason to do so. When emphasis is needed, use *italic text* instead. To italicize text using Microsoft Word, highlight the desired words, then click the italic *I* icon in the Word toolbar.

Use single punctuation marks only, especially for question marks and exclamation points. In rare cases, you may use more than one, but never more than three!!!

Avoid for common writing errors that appear in print all too often:

- "It" is the only word we know that doesn't need an apostrophe in the possessive case. "It's" is strictly a contraction of "it is" and not a possessive. Example of improper usage: "The book revealed it's weaknesses from the first page."

- Except for the special case above, apostrophes are needed for possessives and contractions only, but *not* for plurals. Example of incorrect usage: "Several page's in the book had mistake's."

- The word "They're" is strictly a contraction of "they are" and does not indicate ownership. The word "their" indicates ownership but not location. The word "there" indicates location but not ownership. Example of improper usage: "Their making mistakes in they're writing." Check your manuscript carefully for correct usage of these words throughout.

- The words "to," "two" and "too" sound alike, but mean different things. "Too" means "and" or "as well." Sometimes "to" is incorrectly used in lieu of "too," as in "I'm writing a book to."

- Check the entire manuscript for subject-verb agreement. In brief, when a sentence includes more than one noun, the verb must be plural. To illustrate with an extreme example from a conversation in a restaurant: "Peanut butter and jelly is a good choice." Strictly speaking, if it didn't apply to name of a sandwich, this sentence should read "Peanut butter and jelly are good choices." In common usage the first version is fine. It is cited here simply as an example of the formal rules.

Again, the examples above are elementary and not a substitute for qualified editing. If you find any of them in your manuscript, be sure to get editorial support!

Another helpful note: Microsoft Word often underlines potential grammar and spelling problems in red or green.

Another inside tip: finish your writing and editing 100% (better still 110%) before you start laying out the interior of your book. You will discover that making changes after design work starts is much more costly and time-consuming than polishing the manuscript beforehand.

Take your time writing. Rushing a manuscript to print almost always results in oversights that authors and publishers regret later.

Before publication, you will also need to choose a publishing method, and an initial printing method, which will influence how the manuscript is prepared for publication. Several different options for publishing and printing are discussed in the following chapters.

Chapter 4: Publishing Methods: Self-Publishing Versus Vanity Publishing

Before we turn to *printing*, let's discuss *publishing*. They are not synonyms. There are several forms of publishing, and each one of them may involve different printing methods.

A traditional "royalty" publisher buys the rights to a book from an author, who is generally not involved extensively in design, production or distribution. The writer invests only time (not money) but receives only a small percentage of the publisher's revenues.

A self-publishing author typically engages an editor, book designer, printer, and (if appropriate) a wholesale distributor, each compensated separately. The author invests both time and money, but retains the profits — usually much more per book than paid by a conventional publisher.

A vanity press usually charges the writer for a service package, possibly bundling editing, book design, printing, distribution and sometimes promotion. The writer invests both time and money, but rarely recovers the investment.

There's also a middle ground between royalty publishing and vanity publishing called subsidy publishing, where the author and the publisher share expenses and revenues.

These overlapping factors create a fuzzy picture. What exactly is a vanity press? And how does vanity publishing differ from self-publishing?

The best way to attempt a distinction between vanity publishing and self-publishing is to ask a simple question: *where does the publisher earn money?* From readers or writers? Vanity publishers make more money from fees paid by authors than from book sales.

For writers who have limited computer skills, or limited time, it might make sense to use a vanity or subsidy press. To be fair, it's certainly possible for a vanity press to publish a quality book. But authors who use vanity presses should be aware that the cost of achieving professional quality may prove much higher than expected. For many writers, self-publishing is a better option.

Unless you have more money than time, or you lack basic computer skills, you can probably publish a better book and promote it more effectively on your own.

The following chapters will show you how.

Chapter 5: Printing Methods: POD, Digital Short Run and Offset Printing

Print-on-Demand (POD) is a hot topic in today's world of publishing. Surprisingly, the basic concept isn't new: retailers of household goods like Walmart have used "Just-in-Time" (JIT) inventory management for years. JIT links each store's cash registers with a warehouse or distribution center. When a customer buys an item, a replacement is automatically ordered from the warehouse. POD simply takes JIT to the next level, both manufacturing *and* shipping the product as ordered by consumers.

The core principle of POD is for public demand to *pull* books into the marketplace, unlike the traditional publishing practice of printing books first, then trying to *push* them to readers.

On one hand, POD is a method of printing with toner rather than ink — but it is also a business model like JIT: printing real books in quantities literally as small as one at a time, as they are ordered by readers. Instead of printing thousands of books first, then hoping that readers buy them, the reverse is true: readers order first, then the books are quickly printed and delivered in a matter of days (not weeks) to the buyers. In other words, waste is practically eliminated — you print only as many books as you really need, with few (if any) unsold copies left over. In this section, we use the term "POD" for the business model, and "digital printing" for the production process.

Traditional offset lithography is the best method for printing thousands of books at a time, at the lowest possible per-unit cost. Offset printing is also superior for books with photographs inside, though its lead in halftone reproduction is shrinking.

Digital short-run printing is a middle ground between offset and POD, usually best for runs of 200 to 1,000 copies.

POD is best for printing fewer than 200 copies at a time. We predict that it will become the norm for most books other than sure-fire bestsellers within the next few years.

In a culture of instant gratification, POD books may lose a few sales to readers who don't want to wait even a few days to receive a book — but this is still far better than printing hundreds or thousands of books that don't sell. Moreover, as more and more consumers buy books online and expect to wait a few days for delivery, the difference between POD books and others is diminishing.

Most vanity presses today use digital printing, but that doesn't mean that it is merely for vanity publishing. Real publishers use it too.

According to a leading digital printer, LightningSource, many well-known publishing houses have used POD, including Bantam Doubleday Dell, Cambridge University Press, Columbia University Press, Farrar Straus & Giroux, Grove Atlantic Press, Harcourt Trade, Harper Collins, Henry Holt & Company, McGraw-Hill, NYU Press, Oxford University Press, Penguin Putnam, Random House, Scholastic Books, Simon & Schuster, St. Martins Press, and Time Warner Book Group.

This is a digitally-printed POD book. Although earlier editions were also printed in bulk with ink, few readers notice the difference.

The self-publisher has several options for printing, ranging from POD to produce one book at a time, to digital short run for hundreds, to traditional offset printing for thousands. In this context, they are *printing* processes, rather than *publishing* processes.

You may use one printing method to get started with a small initial quantity, then shift methods as volume increases. It is increasingly possible to migrate almost seamlessly from one production method to another. In previous editions of this book, we made more strict distinctions between POD, digital short run printing, and traditional offset lithography. Today, the differences are diminishing: POD is becoming more competitive in quantities of 100 or more, while short-run printers are starting to offer quantities as small as 200 books at a time. Offset printing is still best for printing thousands, but the lines between printing methods are beginning to blur. The key is to use the method best suited for the quantity you need at any given time.

The ability to scale up from a small initial printing in response to proven demand is a great advantage for the self-publisher, slashing start-up expenses while avoiding costly overstocks.

Self-publishers may find that the same files used to print their POD book often work well for digital short run or offset printing, with little or no modification.

The following chapter provides tips on preparing a manuscript for optimal results using any of the printing methods available.

Chapter 6: From Manuscript to Galley

Whether you choose self-publishing, subsidy publishing or a vanity press (and a suitable printing method), let's assume at this point that you've finished writing, and give your 110% completed manuscript to a book designer to start preparing for printing.

Your designer should know your goals from the start, along with specifications from your printer to achieve the lowest possible print cost, such as ideal trim size and page count. The designer's work will also be influenced by the printing and publishing methods you chose in the previous chapters.

If it is late in the year (September through December) use the following year for the copyright and publication date, and shoot for a January release. This avoids a situation where the book shows the previous year of publication in January, making it appear old, when it is actually new.

Work with the designer to make the cover eye-catching, and market-oriented. On the cover, emphasize why readers benefit from buying. The author's biography can go *inside* the book, reserving valuable "real estate" on the cover to convince readers to buy. Remind the designer to save space for endorsements from VIPs or book reviewers, as we will explain shortly.

Arrange to have some copies printed as soon as the design is completed, for your use in proofreading, and for sending advance copies to reviewers.

While you are waiting for the design to be completed, consult the book titled *Literary Marketplace* at your local library and compile a list of publications that might write a review. You can find others in "Poynter's Secret List of Book Promotion Contacts" (Document 112) and "Book Promotion Mailing Lists" (Document 142) at ParaPublishing.com. Emphasize those with a clear, direct focus on the subject matter of your book. Note the submission policy of each publication: some prefer to receive a galley proof; others prefer a finished book. Send a query letter, fax or e-mail offering a pre-publication copy, before you actually send a book. Be sure to mention the projected publication date, which should be at least 60 to 90 days in the future, because many reviewers require copies well in advance of public release.

Always contact a specific person (rather than a generic address like "Book Review Editor") and address them by name. If additional research is needed to get a specific name, it is well worth the extra time and effort.

Explain why your book is special, but keep your pitch brief and factual. Most reviewers are more receptive to objective reasons (statistics, demographics, references to credible sources) to review a book, than subjective ones. For example, a statement like "This is the first book about middle-eastern mapmaking in the English language" is more persuasive than "This is a very interesting book about middle-eastern mapmaking."

Each advance copy you send to a reviewer costs money, so offer copies only to those who are realistically likely to review your book. You may also want to limit advance copies to reviewers who request them, versus sending "blind" (unsolicited) copies that may never be read. When you ship advance copies to reviewers on request, include "REQUESTED MATERIAL" on the shipping label, to distinguish your book from the blind copies sent by others.

Reviewers are often swamped with offers of new books, and their request to receive an advance copy does *not* guarantee that a review will be published. Do not pester reviewers after you send their advance copies. If a review does not appear within 60 days, you may want to ask for confirmation that they *received* the book, and mention that public release is approaching... but do not pressure them by asking if or when a review will appear.

In some cases, a prospective reviewer may be willing to accept an "e-Galley," which is an electronic copy of the book in Adobe's PDF format. (See the following chapter for details.) A PDF file can be transmitted to a reviewer in moments, at practically no cost to you. PDF files can also provide search capability, and many allow reviewers to copy and paste excerpts to a report or review without re-typing. When reviewers or reporters express interest in your book, offer them a PDF copy first, emphasizing that it is faster and makes their job easier. Although many will still want a printed copy, it is worthwhile to offer a PDF copy first.

As advance copies are sent, determine how you will distribute your book. This report focuses on marketing directly to readers through "non-traditional" channels. But some books need book trade distribution. For example, if your book is scholarly or a reference work, you will probably want to cultivate library orders. Libraries place more than 70% of their orders with wholesalers.

In this case, you will want to make arrangements for trade distribution in advance. Trade distribution is also required if you want readers to order from chain bookstores, Amazon, etc.

For trade distribution, you will need an International Standard Book Number (ISBN) and possibly a Library of Congress Control Number (LCCN) and/or Catalog-in-Publication (CIP) data, which will become part of the book design.

Information about applying for an ISBN is available from R.R. Bowker (Bowker.com). Details about LCCN applications and CIP data may be obtained from the Library of Congress (LOC.gov). Your book will also need a barcode with the ISBN on the cover of the book. See Dan Poynter's "Secret List of Book Promotion Contacts," free at ParaPublishing.com, for advice about barcodes.

You can make arrangements for trade distribution during the two or three months between the galley proof and public release.

If you plan to use direct mail, prepare your materials in advance during this period. As you will see repeatedly in this book, *the key is accurate targeting more than large numbers*. For detailed instructions on selling books by direct mail, see Dan Poynter's special report titled *Direct Mail for Book Publishers* at ParaPublishing.com and mail only to those who have a clear, direct interest in your subject.

To promote his *Expert Witness Handbook*, Poynter rented 4,400 addresses from the *Forensic Services Directory*. The names listed were ALL expert witnesses who had paid to be included in the directory. Because the targeting was accurate, the response to the mailing was better than 11%.

It is much better to send a smaller, carefully targeted mailing than a larger mailing with less direct interest. If possible, start with a small test mailing of 200 pieces sent by bulk mail. Calculate the response rate from the test mailing to insure that future mailings will more than cover your expenses.

Ideally, your test results will also inform your decision about how many books to print initially, as covered in the following chapters. It is a huge advantage to accurately project the number of books you can sell before you start printing.

Create a Web site for your book before it is released. Make sure it is a permanent Web location that is registered in your name. Do not use a Web address that is tied to your Internet Service Provider, such as AOL, Earthlink or a local company, because it could be lost if you change services later. A domain registered to you is "portable," and can be hosted anywhere.

A Google search for "Web Hosting" will help you find companies that offer domain registration and hosting. An annual registration fee of $10 to $20 is typical; hosting fees vary more widely, depending on the size and complexity of your site.

Make sure that your Web address appears prominently in the book. Offer a sample chapter or excerpts online as a free preview. Tell visitors how to order.

Create a "synergy" between your site and your book. At your Web site, emphasize why readers benefit from buying the book. In your book, emphasize why readers benefit from visiting your Web site. More ideas for developing synergies are discussed in the chapter on online promotion.

Highlight your Web location on your letterhead, business cards, and in every e-mail message you send.

Be sure your Web site includes an online "press kit" with a sample book cover, your picture, bio, and excerpts that can be used in reports about the book after it is published. If your subject is related to hot topics in the news, include recent reports, and keep them updated. Invite members of the press to contact you directly with questions.

Your goal is to make it easy for journalists to compose articles by providing them with all the materials they typically need for an article. By making the reporter's job easier, you increase your chance of coverage. Getting media coverage is discussed at greater length later in this report.

Some self-publishing authors use an online service like Paypal.com to accept payments, but ship books to buyers themselves. If you take this approach, consider offering *autographed* copies, which add value for readers.

For orders you ship to readers, you may pass all or part of shipping and handling costs along to buyers. The better choice depends on your personal situation and profit margins. If you have a paperback novel, it may be difficult to command a $20 cover price plus $5 for shipping. On the other hand, legal and medical books often command such high cover prices that shipping is included. Either way, *you must keep the total cost to readers competitive* with similar books from traditional publishers.

Notify personal contacts and others who have a special interest in the subject of your upcoming book that it will become publicly available in the next few months. Some may want to reserve a copy from the first printing in advance.

All the steps above should be well underway by the time your galley proof is ready, as covered in the next chapter.

Chapter 7: From Galley to Book

When the galley is ready, several important steps follow. This phase of self-publishing is the most time sensitive, so it pays to have a calendar, names and addresses, and other materials prepared beforehand.

Anticipate delays, especially if this is your first book. Allow extra time for proofreading, making changes to the book design, printing, shipping, etc., even if you have confidence in your service provider(s). Remember the 90/90 rule of project planning: "The first 10% of the job takes 90% of the time. The rest takes another 90%." On a more serious note, keep in mind that your book might stay in distribution for years; it is much better to take extra time before public release to avoid oversights that could haunt you long afterward.

Quickly send copies to book reviewers who responded to your query letter described earlier. Include a one-page "fact sheet" that details why your book is special, where readers can obtain it, and bibliographic data such as ISBN, page count, binding, retail price, etc.

If you are fortunate enough to know experts in your field, or celebrities with public name recognition, send additional copies of the galley with a request for their comments.

Check the galley carefully for problems. Don't overlook seemingly obvious errors like missing pages. Triple-check the barcode and registration numbers (if any) on the back cover and copyright page to make sure that they are accurate.

At this point it is often helpful to bring in an outsider who knows nothing about the book. An extra set of eyes will sometimes notice things that insiders do not. Authors are often so close to their books that they overlook problems a stranger might find obvious.

Assuming your Web site is up and running by now, start accepting "Advance orders" from readers. If you are fortunate to get many orders in advance, it will help you decide how many books to print initially... and help pay for your initial printing. We've heard more than one story about savvy self-publishers who managed to get enough pre-publication orders to cover the entire cost of publication — including editorial support, book design and an initial printing — before even a single book was printed! In a case like this, you're in the black from Day One, and every subsequent sale simply increases your profits.

You may want to assure readers who order in advance that their checks will not be cashed (or credit cards will not be billed) before their books ship. Think of them as a "savings account" that will help cover the cost of the first printing.

After making corrections and changes from the galley, your designer will soon be ready to send files to the printer. But how many copies should you print? Certainly you will need 100 or more for book reviewers, VIPs, reporters, and early public orders. But we always recommend starting with the smallest realistic quantity.

The single reason self-publishers most often lose money is because of overprinting before actual public demand is proven. Of course we understand that you believe in your book and expect to sell zillions of copies. That's great; if you didn't, why would you publish it at all? But good books don't always enjoy good sales, so please be conservative at first, until you have solid, *objective proof* that larger numbers are actually needed. Remember: you can always print more!

A final note of caution: you will probably notice that the printing cost per book drops dramatically from one copy to 100 copies to 1,000 copies. For a short paperback, your printer might charge $500 or less for 100 copies, but $2,000 or less for 1,000... slashing the per-unit cost more than half. *But what if you need only 200 copies?* In this scenario, you are left with 800 unsold books at $2 each — ouch! *It is MUCH better to pay $5 each for 200 books you really need, versus $2 each for 800 books that don't sell!* Start small. If the first printing sells out, you can always print more next time.

If you are working with a professional designer, your book will probably go to the printer in Adobe's "Portable Document Format" or PDF. The printer will usually want "press-optimized" (or "print optimized") files, which are robust, high-resolution files that are ideal for printing. But sometimes high-resolution files are too big to transmit quickly over the Internet. For this reason, ask the designer to also prepare a "Web-optimized" (or "screen-optimized") set of PDF files that are small enough for online use.

Also remember that PDF files can be modified for different kinds of printing, depending on the quantity you need at any given time.

As we will discuss in the following chapters, in the 21st Century the savvy independent publisher increasingly thinks of a book as both a printed product and a digital or electronic one. There are good uses for both, and they are becoming increasingly interchangeable, depending on your needs at any given time. But first, let's focus on the printed book in the following chapter.

Chapter 8: In Print at Last

Finally, your book is in print! For many writers, holding the first copy of a book in their hands is a defining moment in life. Savor it. Then roll up your sleeves, because the real work of self-publishing is just beginning!

Save a handful of copies from the first printing for yourself. If the book takes off, you'll enjoy having a few of the earliest copies on hand.

Earlier, you may have received requests from book reviewers who prefer finished books, rather than copies of the galley. Mail review copies right away, because reviewers prefer "fresh" books. Depending on the policies of the specific reviewers, you may even want to delay public release for an additional month or two after sending review copies to give reviewers more lead time.

Offer copies to newspapers, radio and TV stations in your geographic area, as well as the publications of schools you attended, magazines of professional associations of which you are a member, or other media with which you have a personal connection. Send a brief query letter that explains the connection; offer excerpts, interviews, live appearances or other benefits to those who cover the book's publication.

Offer additional copies to print and broadcast media that focus on subjects closely related to your book, whether local or distant. Offer print media the right to excerpt from the book, or to serialize chapters. Offer broadcast media live interviews.

Emphasize why your book is newsworthy, and how they can contact you for expert commentary in future reports.

For extensive resources to help cultivate media coverage, please visit:

U-Publish.com/promote and other sources

Book reviews and media coverage may be the best ways to promote books. They are better than advertising. First of all, media coverage is free. In addition, the public finds reviews and reports more credible than advertising.

"Do not spend money on paid advertising until you have exhausted every source of free exposure available!"
— Dan Poynter

If you received advance orders, ship them promptly, with a note of thanks and a request to tell others that the book is finally out. Media Mail from the USPS is a good shipping method for single copies, currently about $2 for the first pound (roughly the weight of a 250-page paperback) with delivery confirmation. Use a sturdy padded envelope to avoid damage to the book in transit. Another option is Priority Mail, about $4 for a flat rate envelope.

Donate one copy to each library, school, church or other organizations in your area that might invite you to hold a live event, and notify local media that you have done so. Offer to do readings, signings, workshops, seminars, etc.

Note that bookstores are not included above. This is because most bookstores (especially the major chains) prefer to buy books from wholesaler distributors, expect big discounts, full returnability and a long time to pay. At other locations, you can sell directly to readers for better earnings. Remember that we are focusing on non-traditional marketing here, through outlets beyond the conventional book industry, as we will discuss shortly.

This is not to say you can't offer copies to local bookstores, especially independents. Just remember that customary bookstore terms are far less favorable than direct sales to readers, or to retailers outside the conventional book trade.

If you are working with a wholesaler, ask your printer to ship their books directly. Store your own in a cool, dry place. Moisture is bad for books, as are variations in temperature. If they are delivered in cartons, leave the cartons unopened and stored on a firm, flat surface. You may want to place a board on top of the cartons and weigh it down for extra firmness.

The steps above are all important at the time of publication, but you will return to them again and again, as we discuss later. Beforehand, let's take a closer look at the options for marketing self-published books in both traditional and non-traditional markets, in the following chapters.

Chapter 9: Traditional Markets

Now that the book has been publicly released, it's time to start promoting it. If you are serious about reaching a broad audience, you must commit yourself to regular, active efforts to cultivate readers, week after week. We've heard stories of *authors who spent years writing their books*, only to quit when their work was finally in print. Is it any wonder they were disappointed by poor sales? How sad... and how silly! Books don't sell themselves.

Writers who have been published the traditional way can attest that the author does the lion's share of promotional work. The same is true for self-published books, except that we emphasize promoting them in non-traditional markets.

Donna Woolfolk Cross, author of *Pope Joan*, sold more than 100,000 copies of her book using grassroots marketing methods, "with only minimal involvement by her publisher."
— *The New York Times*, 5/28/2001

Promoting a book can involve as much creativity as writing one. If you are creative and diligent in your marketing, almost any good book with a clear audience can be promoted effectively. The key is to find readers likely to have real interest, and to contact them directly.

Earlier, we introduced the differences between traditional book trade markets (mostly bookstores and libraries) versus non-traditional markets, such as stores that specialize in products related to the subject of your book, live events, etc.

Customary book trade terms are far less advantageous, but some new writers feel it's "sexy" to say their books are available to order from major bookstores, Amazon, etc. Please weigh the decision to pursue traditional book trade channels carefully, based on more objective criteria.

Chain bookstores expect big discounts, a long time to pay, and the right to return unsold books for a full refund. Traditional publishers often see 20% or more of the books ordered by chain stores returned.

"Bookstores are not the only places to sell books. They aren't even good places to sell books. In fact, bookstores are lousy places to sell books."
— Dan Poynter, *Book Marketing: A New Approach*

Of course, some books truly need trade distribution. As we mentioned earlier, if your book is scholarly or a reference work, marketing to libraries could be essential — and libraries order more than 70% of their books through traditional distribution channels. In this case, you will probably need a wholesale distributor, but remember that their sales will not be as profitable as those you make yourself.

If you want to market your book to libraries, get *Book Marketing: A New Approach* from ParaPublishing.com for more detail about how to cultivate library orders.

Returning to our general discussion of the traditional book trade, the terms "wholesaler" and "distributor" are often used interchangeably. They are the middlemen between the publisher and the bookstore. Technically, wholesalers stock books for several publishers on a non-exclusive basis. They do not push specific books with sales reps and most place orders with publishers only when they receive an order from a bookstore or library. Distributors act like an arm of the publisher. They usually represent publishers on an exclusive basis, warehouse books, and send sales reps to the stores to push the specific titles they carry. For more information about wholesale distributors, see:

www.U-Publish.com/distribute

The important point is that every link in the book trade supply chain takes a percentage. A typical scenario is that the wholesaler or distributor pays the publisher about 50% of cover price, and in turn sells to retailers at a smaller discount. This leaves you, as a self-publisher, with 50% of cover price *less the cost of printing...* for only a modest profit on each sale, even if there are NO returns.

You may respond, "But a modest profit is better than none at all," and you'll be right. However, you should carefully calculate your income after discounts and printing costs before deciding whether to focus on traditional book trade channels or to pursue non-traditional outlets.

Whether you use a wholesale distributor or not, do everything you can to cultivate orders directly from readers at live events, at your own Web site, and from businesses other than bookstores. Accepting orders directly from the public is more beneficial, whether your marketing plans include traditional book trade channels or not.

The following chapters explain the many advantages of outlets beyond bookstores and libraries, and give you tips for cultivating non-traditional markets more effectively.

Chapter 10: Non-Traditional Markets

Remember our earlier example of a book about organic fertilizers? While relatively few bookstore customers are interested, nearly *all* of the customers of a tree nursery or gardening center are potential readers.

It is difficult to predict the specific interests of bookstore customers. Bookstores also expect big discounts, pay slowly, and return unsold books routinely. Outlets beyond the traditional book trade are easier to target and more profitable.

The tree nursery will probably pay more, pay faster, and return fewer (if any) unsold books. Offer them a dozen copies to start, at 20% to 30% below cover price on consignment. If they sell the first dozen on consignment, you have proof of the book's appeal. Offer two dozen more at a bigger discount, COD. Check back periodically to make sure they have enough stock; it seems odd, but retailers sometimes forget to re-order, or to increase quantities to keep up with demand.

Additional non-traditional markets to pursue include live events held at libraries, schools, churches and other locations in your area, bulk sales to businesses and institutions that focus on related topics, and of course, your personal contacts.

Don't be shy about offering your book to people you know personally, especially those named in the acknowledgements. Many will be delighted to see their names in print, and eager to obtain a copy. Church groups, trade associations, social clubs, civic groups, fraternities, alumni associations of schools you attended and other organizations with which you are affiliated are also good prospects. Contact all of them.

At live events, readers often pay full price for books, usually in cash, and of course there are no shipping or handling expenses. Compare these terms to those from traditional book trade outlets, which often order at 50% below cover price, take months to pay, and return unsold books routinely.

At live events it is customary for authors to autograph books. Collectors prefer books that are autographed with a Sharpie marker, and often want only the author's signature on the title page, without an inscription. General readers, however, will often ask the author to inscribe a personal note.

If your book gives positive treatment to a product, service, company or other institution, offer them copies, and ask them to help promote the book to their contacts. In the movie *E.T.*, the extraterrestrial's fondness for Reese's Pieces was worth *millions* to the candy manufacturer. You may be delighted to get significant support from those mentioned favorably in your book.

Here again, the key is a good match between the subject of the book and the institutional buyer. For example, if your book is about investing, talk to local banks, stock brokerages, and other financial institutions that might want copies for their customers as a gift or premium. If the topic of your book is safety, talk to insurance companies and insurance agents who benefit when their customers avoid accidents and injuries. Ask yourself "Which businesses could profit when their customers read my book?" There are probably several in your community that will consider your proposal.

"Multi-Purposing" for Special Markets

Now that your paperback is published, why not offer it several more ways, to make it more attractive to readers with special needs? Dan Poynter calls this "multi-purposing," and it is the heart of his New Book Model.

To illustrate: a growing number of books and reports by Poynter & Snow are becoming available in audio formats.

Why? Because a fundamental strategy we follow is to make our work available in as many formats as possible. Some of our "readers" are simply too busy to read our printed materials... but they do have time to listen to them on the run, whether on tape, CD or by MP3 download.

New technologies now make it possible to create a paperback, hardback, Large Print edition, e-Book, audio book and other formats... all from the same manuscript. *You've already written the book, by far the hardest and most important part of publishing.* Why not give your readers more options to suit their specific needs? More choices means more sales!

Large Print books are another good example. Go back to the PDF file used for your 6x9" paperback, and ask your designer to simply expand it to 8.5x11" with smaller margins. The resulting increase in type size makes it *much* more readable... without changing the page numbers, Table of Contents, etc.

Suppose there are several books about a subject similar to yours... *but only yours is available in enlarged text and audio formats!* Now imagine a busy commuter who drives constantly, or a visually impaired reader who is interested in the subject — whose book do you think will be chosen?

Electronic books are good for reaching foreign readers who may live in locations where shipping a printed book is slow or expensive. Podcasting is a growing trend that allows self-publishers to deliver their content to a "reader's" iPod, cell phone or hand-held PDA device.

How about a hardback edition for schools and libraries? Or a coil-bound "workbook" edition that lays flat on a desk?

Be creative and ask yourself what kind of changes might add value for different kinds of readers, then deliver them.

Self-publishers enjoy an advantage in specialty markets. Use your intimate understanding of your audience to identify specialty markets, and make your book available in formats that give it a competitive edge.

Depending on your subject, you may find many good outlets for special editions in your own community. But your marketing need not be limited to local outlets. That's why the Internet is crucial to self-publishers. The following chapter explains why.

Chapter 11: Online Marketing

As explained earlier, the Web location for your book should appear on the cover, your letterhead, business cards, and in every e-mail message you send.

Invite potential readers to your Web site. A simple Google search on the topic of your own book will often identify *thousands* of sites that focus on related subjects. Visit them one-by-one, and make sure that each site is clearly related to your book. If so, look for a link that reads "Contact Us" and send a brief announcement.

Important: always send announcements *individually*, and *address each recipient by name*: "Dear Mr. Smith, after visiting your Web site, I thought you might be interested in my new book." Do NOT send unsolicited, unwanted, generic form letters (spam) to many addresses at once. Taking the time and effort to personalize each message will pay off in the long run. Once again, accurate targeting of your audience is more important than raw volume. It's better to contact a dozen people who are truly interested than 100 who are not.

Make your own Web site equally easy for others to find using search engines. BruceClay.com has an extensive set of resources to help give your site better visibility with search engines. Google.com is the most important, but Yahoo.com, MSN.com and "meta-engines" like DMOZ.org are also worthwhile. Register your site by hand at each search engine, rather than using an automated submission service. Re-register every month or two, to insure that they have current information. We do not normally recommend paying for search engine placement, since "sponsored links" are often considered suspect by the public, and because the ratio of sales per click is usually very low.

Newsgroups are also a good tool for getting the word out about your book. Visit Groups.Google.com and join groups related to your subject. Here again, *do not* post "off-topic," blatantly commercial announcements. Instead, participate in earnest, and post only items that are truly relevant to the groups you join. It's fine to mention that you are the author of a book on a related topic, but make your posts more than just a sales pitch.

At your own site, create a meaningful incentive for visitors to *give you their contact information*, whether they buy the book or not. One good method is to offer a free e-mail newsletter or other information of real value that is not contained in the book itself. For example, this book refers to several lists of services for self-publishers that change frequently, as new ones appear, others change addresses and so forth. We maintain them at our Web site, so you can get current information long after the book goes to press, and we invite you to sign up for free monthly updates sent by e-mail. You may want to offer a different incentive or freebie... but the point is to *gather names and addresses of visitors* for subsequent use.

Do not give personal information about visitors to your site to others, and make sure visitors know that you will respect their privacy.

The benefits of collecting contact information are significant. For example, you might write another book in the future... wouldn't it be great to contact your current readers when the new book is released? Or future developments in the news might suddenly heighten interest in your subject, giving you a reason to re-contact reviewers and reporters with expert commentary.

This is yet another advantage of marketing directly to the public. When readers buy books at most retail outlets, you get less income, and NO contact info. Online booksellers certainly collect info on book buyers — but they don't share it with you! We suggest that you "flip the script" and give readers real incentives to order from you directly, whether you offer an autographed copy, free updates, or other benefits.

Some readers will still order through public channels, and that's fine — but these are an AND rather than an OR. Any sale is a good sale, but orders placed directly from you are better than those placed through middlemen.

If your book has an ISBN and you have distribution channels that serve libraries, contact everyone you know in other locations and suggest they request your book at a local library. Also ask them to forward your invitation to others. This is more tasteful than suggesting that they buy the book, with the added benefit that it will be available to other readers too. Most libraries are receptive to requests from patrons. Many have a "suggestion box" for this purpose, and some even accept suggestions by e-mail or telephone.

There are many other methods of online marketing that might be effective, depending on the subject of your book and your level of computer skill. Experiment according to your personal situation, and use the ones that work best.

For an extensive list of book promotion tools that are regularly updated, please visit our Web site periodically to get the latest resources:

U-Publish.com/promote and other sources

The key to successful marketing is *persistence*. Commit yourself to spending at least a few hours, week after week, trying new methods and repeating those that produce the best results. The Internet is vast, and you may never reach all the Web locations where prospective readers of your book may be found. Even if you scour the entire Web, before you reach the end, new sites will probably appear elsewhere. It's a perpetually renewable resource, but *you must be diligent in cultivating it*, month after month.

"Book promotion is an on-going process, not a one-time event!"
— Danny O. Snow

No matter how ambitious your initial promotional efforts may be, on-going promotion is crucial. For example, earlier we discussed the benefits of media coverage at the time of publication. But what if future developments in the news suddenly put your subject in the spotlight? Go back to those who reported on your book initially, and remind them about it! Or try again with the journalists who did *not* cover your book the first time. You may be pleasantly surprised to gain new exposure, long after the book is released.

After working with hundreds of authors, we have discovered that *the most successful self-publishers are not necessarily the best writers, but the best promoters. Moreover, the most successful promoters are not necessarily the most persuasive or sophisticated, but the most diligent.*

If you are serious about achieving widespread readership (and good sales!) make a regular practice of looking for new readers, week after week. Our experience tells us that there will be a direct relationship between the number of prospective readers you contact, and the number of books you sell.

You've worked hard getting your book published. Please *give it the chance it deserves to succeed,* by continuing your promotional efforts, online and offline, on a regular basis.

Chapter 12: Afterword

Online or offline, Dan Poynter says the key is to "think outside the book." On an impulse, he once offered a carton of books about self-publishing to a local instant print center. Apparently writers do a lot of instant printing, because the books soon sold out, and the center ordered more. Now Dan supplies many printing and copying centers with his books, as a regular part of his business.

Use your imagination. If you have a new idea, try a small test and see if it works. You may be pleasantly surprised when an unusual idea takes off.

Make a list of *every possible* public or private institution, print or broadcast medium, business or individual with potential interest in your book. Contact each of them individually and explain why, with each proposal specifically tailored to the needs of the recipient.

Ask yourself *"Who benefits when people read my book?"* Then contact every one who benefits and get them involved.

Throughout this report, we've emphasized the benefits of creating synergies between printed and digital content. We do this too. Please visit U-Publish.com for ongoing updates, additions, corrections, and other features to help keep you informed after you've finished reading this book.

One of the greatest benefits of self-publishing is that authors are *passionate* about their subjects, and know their specific markets better than most book industry people. A traditional publisher or bookseller might know (or care) very little about your book's topic; to them, your book is just one more faceless product among thousands of others. But the author is a *participant*. As someone actively involved in a specific field, you probably follow the publications and broadcasts that cover your topic, attend related events, and know others who share your interests. Harness your more intimate understanding of the subject and its audience, and you can do a better job of marketing and promotion than an outsider who sees your book as a "product" rather than a passion.

More and more writers today are bypassing publishers, and the traditional book trade, in favor of reaching readers directly. New methods for the production, distribution and promotion of books make independent publishing more effective and economical than ever before. In the years ahead, many thousands more authors will publish their own books successfully. You can be one of them.

— DFP and DOS, September 2006

Appendix: The "Living Book"

We call this new edition a "living book" because we will use new technologies to keep readers up-to-date long after it goes to press. Fresh new information is added month after month, via the Web, e-mail and with on-demand printing.

Readers who obtained this edition from a chain bookstore or from one of the leading online booksellers can get free monthly updates at the Web site named for the book:

www.U-Publish.com/monthly.htm

We have also made a special arrangement with Lulu.com to update the paperback edition on a monthly basis, starting in January 2007. If you obtain a copy from Lulu thereafter, the following pages will contain fresh new material from our newsletters, added throughout the year.

Whether you prefer Web, e-mail or print, we hope you find that our "Living Book" strategy helps keep you informed about the latest developments in self-publishing for years to come.

Also by Dan Poynter

The Self-Publishing Manual:
How to Write, Print and Sell Your Own Book

Writing Nonfiction:
Turning Thoughts into Books

Successful Nonfiction:
Tips & Inspiration for Getting Published

The Expert Witness Handbook:
Tips & Techniques for Litigation

Parachuting:
The Skydivers' Handbook

Book Marketing:
A New Approach

*Books by Dan Poynter and extensive resources (many free) for
self-publishers are available at ParaPublishing.com.*

Also by Danny O. Snow

Steal this e-Book!
An irreverent collection of articles about electronic publishing

Publish or Perish:
The Professional Public Speaker's Guide to Book Publishing

Above the Fold:
The Working Journalist's Guide to Book Publishing

Books and articles by Danny O. Snow, as well as regular updates to this book, are available at U-Publish.com.

About the Book:

"...A superb manual which makes the case for self-publishing and demonstrates that it is possible to go head to head against the Big Boys and come out a winner... Easy to read and wonderfully complete in its concepts and introductory information, this book is encouraging and truthful. We rated it five hearts."
— Bob Spear, Publisher and Chief Reviewer, *Heartland Reviews*

About the Authors:

"Poynter and Snow: a tremendous team. Both are great writers and they know the publishing business, both electronic and print."
— Randy "Dr. Proactive" Gilbert, Author of *Success Bound*

Dan Poynter is an author of more than 100 books, a publisher since 1969 and a Certified Speaking Professional (CSP). He is an evangelist for books, an ombudsman for authors, an advocate for publishers and the godfather to thousands of successfully published books. His seminars have been featured on CNN, his books have been pictured in *The Wall Street Journal*, and his story has appeared in *U.S. News & World Report*. The media come to Poynter because he is the leading authority on independent book publishing. He travels more than 4,000 miles each week to inspire and empower writers, publishers and professional speakers.

Harvard graduate **Danny O. Snow** has been widely quoted about new publishing technologies by major broadcast and print media, including AP, UPI, NPR, *The Los Angeles Times, The Wall Street Journal* and many others. He has also served as a contributing editor to *BookTech: The Magazine for Publishers*, as a panelist and moderator at national publishing events such as PMA's "Publishing University," as senior planning consultant to Lulu.com, and as a full-time POD book publisher with Unlimited Publishing LLC.

Printed in the United States
66470LVS00007BA/20

9 781588 321756